Introduction:

In the ever-changing world of business, the constant search for new and effective ways to attract customers and promote growth is ongoing. Traditional methods like cold calls, emails, paid advertising, referrals, SEO, social media marketing, content development, conferences, and trade shows have long been the go-to strategies for business development. However, within these familiar tactics are some unconventional approaches that can surprisingly lead to significant success, opening doors to fresh opportunities for growth and increased revenue.

This book is a collection of stories that narrate my journey through the complexities of business growth, spanning from the early stages to becoming an established agency. These stories stray from the typical narratives found in marketing or sales handbooks, providing unique insights that break away from the norm. This book doesn't just highlight my personal achievements or advocate for copying my experiences. Its main purpose is to give you the chance to delve into these anecdotes and find inspiration for yourself. By doing so, my hope is that you find valuable insights and inspiration to adapt and apply to your specific business situation, drawing from my accumulated experience and success. So, let's explore these tales together and uncover lessons that can potentially transform your approach to business growth.

A Little about My Journey:

The initial fifteen years of my career found me deep in the confines of corporate America. From contributing to digital marketing agencies serving Fortune 500 clients to transitioning to the client side and collaborating with a national software company within the expansive environment of a multibillion-dollar consulting firm, my corporate journey was rich with diverse experiences. However, the allure of entrepreneurship beckoned, compelling me to leverage my skills in marketing and sales to establish my own business. This marked the inception of a new chapter, one dedicated to supporting smaller businesses in their sales and marketing endeavors.

For 5 1/2 years, my entrepreneurial venture thrived, weathering the challenges presented by the pandemic and consistently achieving year-over-year growth. While not a behemoth in size, the company demonstrated profitability and maintained revenue figures well into the mid-six figures. The climax of this chapter unfolded in August 2023 when my business was acquired by a national software company, realizing the dream shared by many entrepreneurs and agency founders. Throughout this multi-year odyssey, I not only amassed invaluable business acumen but also underwent personal growth, shaping me as an individual, husband, father, and business owner. Subsequently, I embarked on a new journey by establishing another agency, focusing on similar work in different industries to avoid conflicts with existing non-compete agreements.

Your Journey with this Book:

As you explore the pages of this book, my sincere hope is that it becomes a source of guidance and inspiration in your own entrepreneurial journey. My intention is to stimulate unconventional thinking and novel approaches to marketing and business development, challenging you to broaden your perspectives.

Remember, these stories are not embellished tales; they are authentic and accurate reflections of my experiences. If you'd like a more in-depth exploration of the details, I invite you to connect with me for further discussion. Happy reading!

$100,000 Donuts – 12 Brief Stories of Business Success Through Unconventional Strategies

Table of Contents

Justin Gooderham – Founder, Author, Husband, Father, Friend

#1: The Discovery of Untapped Potential in a Local Convenience Store

As an aficionado of German beers, my quest for unique brews led me to a hidden gem within my neighborhood—a convenience store with an exceptional selection of hard-to-find wines and international beers. Unlike the typical grocery stores carrying mainstream brands, this establishment showcased a distinct section catering to those with more specific tastes.

This particular store, however, lacked an online presence. With an outdated Facebook page and no website, its existence remained largely unknown beyond the local community. Personally stumbling upon this treasure trove, I identified an opportunity to bridge the gap between the store and potential customers through the power of digital marketing.

Engaging in a conversation with the store owner, whom I had befriended over the years, I commended the establishment's international beer selection, noting its uniqueness in comparison to bars and specialty alcohol retailers. Intriguingly, the store also featured a rotating tap, allowing patrons to fill their own growlers—a distinctive offering for a convenience store.

Observing the absence of a website, I pointed out the limitations of relying solely on a Facebook page. Expanding on my role as a local web designer specializing in creating Google search-friendly sites, I illustrated the missed customer opportunities resulting from the store's digital invisibility.

Using a hypothetical scenario, I detailed the potential loss of customers seeking specific beers in the vicinity. The absence of an optimized website meant the store wouldn't appear in Google search results, hindering its visibility and, consequently, losing out on numerous potential customers throughout the year.

Despite the owner's initial reliance on social media, I emphasized the incomparable benefits of a dedicated website in terms of reach and optimization. As our conversation progressed, he became increasingly interested in the possibilities a website could unlock for his business.

Guiding him through my sales process, I delved into his business's pain points, goals, and customer profile. After gauging his needs, I presented a comprehensive quote for a website development project, breaking down the costs and outlining the potential advantages. The owner, recognizing the value of this proposition, promptly agreed, marking the inception of a mutually beneficial partnership.

As I routinely connect with the store owner every few months, or whenever I require a refill of my favorite beers, he consistently expresses satisfaction with the website's performance. On numerous occasions, he has shared with me his delight in gaining new customers who discovered his store through Google searches specifically tailored to the specialty beers he offers—the very ones his website is expertly optimized for.

This narrative serves as a testament to the importance of keen observation, identifying business needs, and effectively communicating the benefits of a tailored solution. In the scope of business, keeping one's senses attuned to opportunities, as demonstrated in this instance, can lead to substantial growth and success. While this particular example may not directly mirror your business, it encourages a thoughtful consideration of how you can identify gaps, provide value, and forge relationships to the benefit of both parties involved.

#2: A Strategic Alliance with a Local Firearm Store

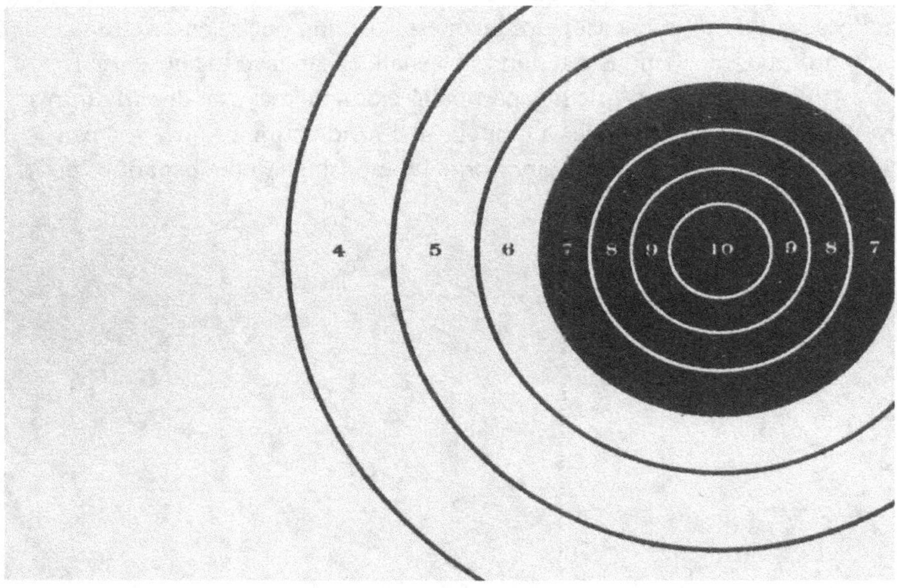

In the midst of navigating the early years of my agency ownership, a moment presented itself when I sought to expand my clientele. Simultaneously, my quest for a new handgun led me to a firearm store located approximately 30 minutes away. This establishment, though not easily discoverable in a standard Google search, caught my attention due to its proximity and potential for collaboration. As I delved deeper, I uncovered a host of issues with their digital presence, including an outdated and non-mobile-friendly website with confusing inventory messaging.

I decided to venture into the store, not only with the intention of making a firearm purchase for my personal use but also to extend a helping hand to the business owner by introducing him to my marketing agency.

Upon entering, I engaged in conversation with a sales associate, sharing insights into my firearm needs and discussing the challenges I faced in navigating their website. This prompted a conversation about the potential of enhancing their online presence through my marketing expertise. Recognizing the significance of addressing these challenges, the sales associate promptly facilitated an introduction to the owner. A valuable side note—always prioritize interactions with the owner, the decision-maker, to streamline the decision-making process and avoid unnecessary delays.

Engaging in a conversation with the owner, I employed my established sales process, diving into questions about the business, its goals, and uncovering pain points. It became evident that the owner lacked technical knowledge and the time to manage a website. Given that a significant portion of internet users conduct searches from mobile devices, an unoptimized website can lead to a poor user experience, rendering the business virtually invisible. Moreover, the potential for Google penalties due to non-mobile-friendly sites further stacked the odds against him.

Seizing the opportunity, I outlined a comprehensive plan to redesign and optimize the website, promising a more user-friendly interface within 30 days. The proposal extended beyond a one-time fix, including ongoing collaboration to add relevant content and optimize the site for Google searches. In a strategic move, we agreed on a barter system, exchanging the handgun I desired for my services in building and enhancing their website. Complementing this arrangement, we also negotiated a cash deal, amounting to $1500 per month, for the ongoing optimization of the website.

Over the subsequent months and years, the business witnessed a remarkable surge in both online website visits and physical foot traffic. Their exclusive online presence expanded, accompanied by a proportional growth in revenue and an expanding customer base. Notably, the owner's satisfaction with our work was so profound that they entrusted our agency with multiple side projects for other affiliated businesses. This gratifying collaboration has since flourished, marking the ongoing growth of our partnership.

This proactive approach and strategic collaboration resulted in approximately $20,000 worth of new business. It underscores the significance of recognizing opportunities, effectively communicating the value proposition of your services, and establishing mutually beneficial partnerships with business owners. As this narrative illustrates, the foresight to engage with a decision-maker, address pain points, and propose viable solutions can lead to substantial and lucrative business outcomes.

#3: The Significance of Proactive Inquiry in Business Development

Justin presenting at a conference

During the early stages of my business, I was constantly exploring avenues to connect with potential clients, particularly small business owners seeking marketing support. Recognizing the efficiency of engaging with multiple prospective clients simultaneously, I sought a strategy that would allow me to achieve this goal. Webinars and in-person educational presentations stood out as effective methods, as observed in the success of other businesses.

In my county, a business economic development group proved to be a goldmine of resources and tools for local business owners. Navigating their website, I accessed valuable information on activities like forming an LLC and obtaining a local business license, critical aspects that were still unfamiliar to me as a budding entrepreneur.

While perusing their website, I discovered a series of monthly speaker events covering diverse topics from finance to legal matters and even marketing. Inspired by the prospect, I reached out to the director of the business development agency, expressing my interest in learning more about their offerings. Enthusiastically, she invited me for a meeting where she provided a comprehensive overview of the group's resources. Capitalizing on the opportunity, I broached the subject of contributing to their event series, proposing a presentation on 'Marketing Must-Haves for Small Businesses." Delighted by the idea, she agreed, and we scheduled the event for six weeks later. The agency committed to handling all marketing aspects and extending invitations to the extensive list of contacts in their network.

During the time leading up to the event, I developed a PowerPoint presentation designed to be informative rather than overtly sales focused. The day arrived, and I had the privilege of sharing my knowledge with an engaged audience of approximately 50 local business owners. They hung on every word, eager to glean insights to enhance their businesses. While I understood that a majority might attempt a DIY approach, I hoped for those few business owners seeking professional assistance.

Post-presentation, I capitalized on the opportunity to personally connect with attendees, shaking hands and introducing myself. Subsequently, I arranged follow-up appointments with four or five of them. Two of these interactions resulted in my first clients, marking a significant milestone for my burgeoning business.

This entire opportunity materialized simply because I proactively requested it. By recognizing the value of a resource that had benefited me and offering to reciprocate by adding value to their membership, a mutually beneficial alliance was forged. It serves as a testament to the profound impact one can achieve in both personal and professional realms through the simple act of asking. Indeed, life has a remarkable way of responding when you articulate your needs and aspirations.

#4: Strategic Engagement at Trade Shows – A Low-Cost Triumph

The saying "Go Where Your Customers Are" may seem commonplace in the realm of sales and marketing. However, I'd like to share a distinctive perspective on how I effectively positioned myself in front of numerous potential customers at minimal cost. In this account, I deviated from the traditional approach of sponsoring conferences and trade shows, opting for a different strategy that yielded outstanding results.

Conferences and trade shows are integral fixtures in the marketing and business development landscape. Typically, companies sponsor these events, set up booths, and engage with attendees as they peruse the offerings. In my case, having clients in the firearms industry, as detailed in a previous story, allowed me to establish my agency as an expert in websites and online marketing tailored to this niche. Rather than relying on conventional methods such as cold outreach, ads, and SEO, I sought a more direct approach to connect with potential customers.

Periodically, a well-attended gun show took place about 30 minutes from my location, with a modest entry fee of $15 for consumers. The show featured numerous tables showcasing firearms companies, vendors, and industry supporters. Recognizing that those sponsoring the event and hosting booths likely invested substantial sums, ranging from several hundred to over $1000, I discerned an opportunity. As an attendee, I could access this vast pool of potential customers in a single afternoon, providing an unparalleled chance to engage with them directly.

With business cards in hand and a refined pitch, I purchased a ticket to the trade show and navigated the tables. Operating on a Thursday evening, the first night of the conference, allowed for a less crowded environment, providing ample opportunities for meaningful conversations. I targeted larger tables with distinctive signage, surmising that these might belong to more established companies capable of affording my services. While avoiding disruptions during customer interactions, I approached vendors who seemed receptive, leveraging the captive audience to introduce myself and my offerings.

Engaging with firearms vendors, I found most to be receptive and open to discussions. As I shared insights into my agency's services and support for the firearms industry, seven companies expressed interest in exploring further. Through my established sales process, I unearthed pain points related to the challenges of paid advertising in an industry restricted by most social platforms and websites. Aware of these limitations, I proposed focusing on search engine optimization and organic social media promotion as viable alternatives to paid advertising.

Furthermore, many vendors expressed dissatisfaction with their websites' mediocre appearance and sought a more professional online presence. Three companies, particularly intrigued by my offerings, agreed to set up follow-up meetings to delve deeper into their specific needs and discuss how my company could aid in their business growth. Collecting business cards and contact information, I secured several meetings on the spot.

In the ensuing weeks, these efforts materialized into six scheduled meetings, with three of them culminating in paying customers generating approximately $20,000 each annually. To put it succinctly, my investment of $15 on a ticket, $10 on business cards, and a mere two hours of my time at the trade show resulted in a remarkable return of about $60,000 in new business.

Over the following years, I collaborated with these new clients to establish a significant online presence, resulting in increased exposure for their businesses and ultimately driving sales growth. Their satisfaction led to referrals within their network, and the impact from that initial trade show continued to yield positive results.

While this approach may not be universally applicable, the key takeaway is to encourage contemplation of unconventional, grassroots strategies that demand little more than strategic thinking and time. In contrast to previous experiences where I spent thousands sponsoring conferences, this method proved equally successful, emphasizing the potential for significant returns with modest investments.

#5: The $100,000 Donuts – A Lesson in Persistence and Creativity

In the world of sales, persistence and creative thinking can sometimes lead to unexpected success. In my agency, which catered to various niches but primarily focused on title insurance companies, I often found myself engaging in conversations and cultivating relationships with owners of such businesses nationwide. My comprehensive sales and marketing strategy involved a multifaceted approach, including conferences, paid advertisements, SEO efforts, and the formidable task of cold outreach – encompassing both email and cold calls.

One particular outreach effort yielded promising results. I had connected with a title insurance company based in the Midwest, and upon inspecting their website, I discovered it was outdated, lacked optimization for Google search, and exhibited a minimal social media presence. Recognizing the potential for my agency to provide substantial support, I engaged in a productive conversation with the owner, providing valuable feedback on how we could enhance their marketing efforts. To my surprise, our discussion unveiled that he wasn't just the owner of one company but held ownership of five distinct title insurance companies spread across the Midwest. I had struck gold with a potential five-client deal – a marketing endeavor to support the diverse brands under his ownership without the need to hire five full-time internal employees.

The excitement of this prospect was palpable, and I swiftly presented pricing details, timelines, and a comprehensive plan that aligned perfectly with their needs. The next step in our journey was for me to send over a proposal and reconvene three days later to either secure a definitive yes or address any lingering questions. However, this promising trajectory took an unexpected turn. For four weeks, the owner failed to attend follow-up meetings and remained unresponsive. Time, an unforgiving force in sales, was slipping away, and my chances of closing the deal were diminishing rapidly.

Faced with the challenge of maintaining engagement without being perceived as an annoying salesperson, I contemplated unconventional ways to rekindle the dialogue. Unsure of the owner's stance – whether he had lost interest, sought alternatives, or encountered unforeseen obstacles – I found myself in limbo with no clear update. It was then that I posed a question to myself: Could I do something out of the ordinary to capture his attention and, at the very least, elicit a response?

Deciding to take an unconventional approach, I opted to send him and his main office a thoughtful gesture – a few dozen donuts from the local Dunkin' Donuts that delivered to his area. The total cost was a modest $60, and I included a note reiterating our previous conversation, expressing our eagerness to support him, and kindly requesting his response. A week passed, and still, silence prevailed. Then, on a Thursday afternoon after business hours, my phone lit up with his contact information. Anticipation coursed through me as I answered the call.

Expressing gratitude for the unexpected donut delivery, the owner apologized for the lapse in communication, revealing that they were undergoing a rigorous audit that demanded their full attention. Acknowledging the multiple priorities that had kept him preoccupied, he commended my consistent follow-up efforts and appreciated the personal touch of the donuts. Remarkably, he declared his readiness to proceed, and within 20 minutes, I secured a signed contract for a five-client multi-deal worth over $125,000 annually. Elation washed over me, knowing that this triumph was a direct result of my persistent yet polite follow-up, coupled with the unique touch of the donut delivery.

In the world of sales, it is often emphasized that fortunes lie in the follow-up, and this experience reinforced that sentiment. People may want to do business with you, but the demands on their time necessitate persistent efforts. Skilled professionals navigate the delicate balance of follow-up until they elicit a response from their prospect. This success story underscores the crucial interplay between persistence, creativity, and strategic engagement in achieving substantial business outcomes. Imagine the missed opportunity had I neglected to follow up at all.

#6: The Art of Bartering – A Win-Win Business Exchange

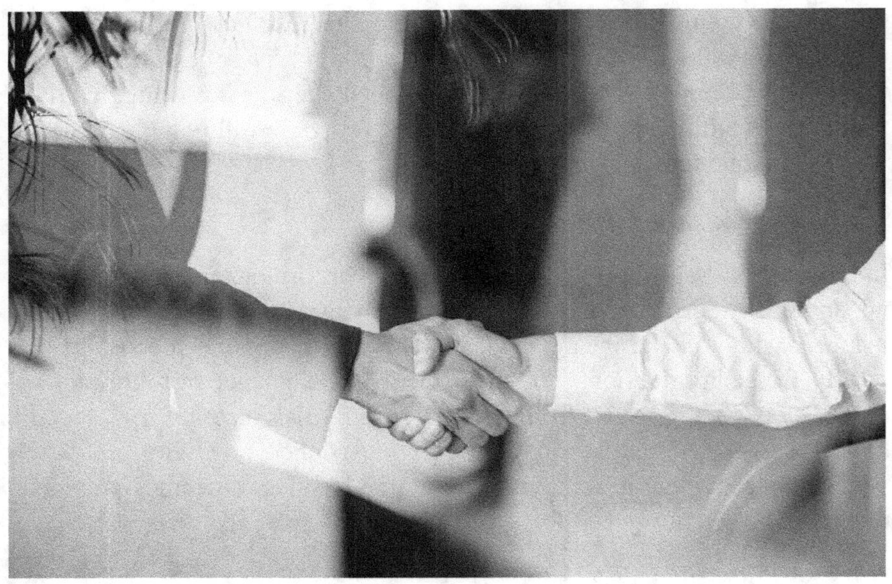

In the early stages of my business, when I was eager to collaborate with any small business, I had yet to narrow down my focus to a specific industry. Simultaneously, I found myself immersed in numerous home renovations, ranging from a new driveway to a remodeled kitchen, as well as a fence for my property. During this time, I encountered a fencing company with reasonable pricing, and after a detailed discussion during the estimate, the final proposal amounted to approximately $10,000.

Seizing the moment, I mentioned to the fencing company owner that I owned a web design company catering to small businesses. His immediate response was enthusiastic, and he expressed a genuine need for web design services. It was at this juncture that I proposed an unconventional yet mutually beneficial arrangement – a barter of services. While acknowledging that our web design services did not command a fee as high as $10,000, I suggested a payment of $5,000 in cash coupled with a barter for the remaining services. During our conversation, he disclosed that his daughter also owned a fencing company in another state and needed a website.

Taking advantage of the opportunity, I offered to build websites for both the fencing company owner and his daughter for the agreed-upon consideration of $10,000, ensuring that no cash would be exchanged. The proposal resonated positively with him, and the barter agreement materialized seamlessly, creating a win-win situation for both parties involved.

Both the client and his daughter continue to leverage the website and work we did many years ago to serve as the front door to their business online. I check in on them periodically and they continually reference their websites to showcase the work that they do for their customers.

This unique experience evoked the spirit of the 1800s, when bartering was a commonplace practice. Reflecting on this transaction, I encourage you to contemplate unconventional avenues for business growth, client acquisition, and compensation. Bartering, though seemingly antiquated, proved to be a remarkably cool and mutually advantageous experience, underscoring the versatility of innovative approaches in business development.

#7: Leveraging Indirect Connections for Business Growth

In a continuation of the theme of conferences, I'd like to share a pivotal experience from a sponsored event in Florida a few years ago. While conferences are renowned for forging new connections and potentially boosting revenue, the success of such endeavors hinges on the presence of the right potential customers. Unfortunately, this was not entirely the case in the conference I attended, as the target market of title insurance companies proved to be scarce. Despite a significant investment in travel accommodations and sponsorship, it appeared that the anticipated returns might not materialize.

After three days of managing my booth at the conference without much traction, I found myself on the brink of considering this venture a less-than-ideal investment. However, a turning point emerged when I engaged in a conversation with another vendor. During our discussion, he brought up a company that was operating as a franchisor for title companies. Essentially, this company offered a turnkey solution for those aspiring to start their own title company. While this specific franchise wasn't directly aligned with my market, the franchisees they catered to presented an ideal customer base for my services.

Prompted by this revelation, I delved into researching this franchise company, identified the owner, and promptly connected with him on LinkedIn. In the subsequent week, I initiated a discussion, conveying that my company specialized in supporting businesses similar to his clients. Recognizing the value of introducing his clients to my services, the owner of the franchise expressed interest. Taking the collaboration a step further, I proposed organizing an informative webinar specifically tailored to address marketing strategies within the title insurance industry for his clients.

With several dozen franchisees as his clients and prospects, the owner took charge of the marketing efforts, disseminating invitations to the webinar. When the webinar unfolded a few weeks later, drawing approximately 25 attendees, I adhered to my standard webinar process and subsequent follow-up routine. This involved reaching out to each webinar attendee via email and phone, extending an offer for a free evaluation and business analysis.

As time progressed, three of the attendees decided to become clients, contributing a total revenue value of about $90,000 to my business. Remarkably, these clients did not originate from the conference itself; instead, they were a product of a chance encounter with a fellow vendor who identified a company I should engage with. Seizing the opportunity, I proactively reached out, scheduled a call, and eventually closed nearly six figures in new business. This story underscores the importance of recognizing indirect benefits even when a particular initiative, such as the conference in this case, may not seem immediately fruitful.

#8 Coffee and Closings

Engaging in cold outreach via email is a well-established strategy in the realm of business development. Many sales and marketing professionals rely on this method to generate leads, piquing interest and, hopefully, closing new deals. While the mass-market approach has its merits, I discovered success by adopting a more focused, hyperlocal tactic, aiming for in-person meetings.

To begin, I curated a list of approximately 25 local title companies that I believed could benefit from my services. Crafting a simple yet compelling email, I introduced myself and inquired if they were interested in growing their business, emphasizing that my company specializes in supporting their industry. To add a personal touch, I devised a clever email subject line: "Coffee and Closings." This choice aimed to resonate with title companies, where the number of real estate files closed each month serves as a benchmark for success. By suggesting an in-person coffee meeting, I anticipated a more personalized approach that would yield positive responses.

The results exceeded expectations. Out of the 25 emails sent, I received 18 responses, demonstrating the effectiveness of the hyperlocal and targeted outreach. Five companies agreed to meet in person within the next two weeks. During these face-to-face meetings, I seamlessly navigated through my sales process. I inquired about their business, unearthed pain points, and ultimately presented my solution to address their specific needs. I successfully closed two deals, totaling about $60,000, within a few weeks of these meetings.

The third deal, however, unfolded at a more measured pace. The prospective client, cautious about investing in marketing amid the fluctuating real estate market, required a more persistent follow-up. As emphasized earlier, fortunes indeed lie in the follow-up. Monthly check-ins, coupled with the delivery of value through blog articles and marketing tips, sustained the interest of this client. Although not ready to commit initially, the consistent engagement eventually paid off. After investing additional effort in crafting a homepage mockup for their desperately needed website makeover, they were convinced and signed off on another five-figure annual contract.

This meticulous, hyperlocal approach to reaching and forming in-person connections with a local audience stands in stark contrast to the mass email strategy. The client appreciated this personalized touch, and the strategy ultimately yielded a substantial return. This success underscores the power of tailored outreach and the value of fostering local connections in business development.

#9: The Benefits of Local Speaking Engagements in Business Development

As discussed in story # 3, engaging in local speaking initiatives not only benefits the community but can also work wonders for your business. Building a positive reputation in the community positions you as a go-to person for business advice, and this became evident when I was invited by my county's economic business development group to participate in a panel discussion about marketing for small businesses, specifically directed at startup business owners.

Initially, I didn't anticipate significant outcomes from this conference, as my focus had not been on startups. To my surprise, the audience included not only startups but also established businesses seeking ways to enhance their growth strategies.

During the 45-minute panel discussion, I shared insights and answered questions, and what followed was an engaging session of one-on-one discussions with attendees. A particular business owner stood out, eager to explore ways to expand her masonry business locally. We delved into the intricacies of her business, discussing its history, the quality of her work, her customer acquisition strategies, and the areas she served. Recognizing the potential, we scheduled a follow-up meeting for the following week, allowing me time to assess her online presence thoroughly and incorporate detailed feedback as part of my sales process.

In her case, she ran an established business with the capacity for growth, aiming to extend her reach beyond a specific radius. After careful consideration, we identified that optimizing her website for Google searches in specific cities aligned with her services was the key. While organic search engine optimization (SEO) typically requires some time to yield results, we explored faster alternatives, given her budget. With the financial capacity to invest in paid Google search ads, we crafted a comprehensive package combining organic and paid advertising. The proposal, including pricing, deliverables, and timelines, gained approval within a few days, with the business owner and her partner signing off on the agreement.

In just a short span of a few months partnering with her, the results have been remarkably rewarding. Their investment has yielded substantial returns, propelling them to secure prominent positions on the initial pages of Google for specific search terms crucial to their business. Notably, they are now experiencing a surge in phone calls and leads from across the region, precisely achieving one of the primary goals outlined in the campaign.

This instance validates the significance of being in the right place at the right time and consistently putting yourself out there where potential customers might be. The invitation to join the panel was a testament to having a prominent local brand. Without it, I wouldn't have had the opportunity to address this audience or connect with businesses looking to enhance their growth strategies. Emphasizing the importance of community involvement, this experience showcases how being seen as a local expert can serve as a catalyst for meaningful business development opportunities.

#10: The Impact of Staying Updated on Industry News for Business Development

Maintaining awareness of the latest developments in your industry proves to be an invaluable strategy for building connections and fostering new business opportunities. A prime example from my experience comes from my time marketing within the title insurance industry. Scrolling through LinkedIn, I stumbled upon news about a new software provider catering to title insurance companies. The attention-grabbing headline highlighted their achievement of surpassing 500 5-star reviews on a prominent review platform, prompting me to delve deeper into this previously unfamiliar entity.

To initiate contact, I sent a congratulatory message to the founder, introducing myself and my company. Unsurprisingly, I received no immediate response to my LinkedIn message. Undeterred, I sought out the company's email on their website and replicated the message, yet still encountered silence. Opting for a more direct approach, I placed a cold call to the founder using the contact number listed on the website, and to my surprise, he answered, paving the way for a fruitful conversation.

During our initial discussion, I conveyed that my company specializes in assisting businesses in the title industry to acquire more clients. Intrigued, he expressed interest, particularly since his company was not actively engaged in marketing efforts at that time. We scheduled a follow-up call for the subsequent week, allowing me the opportunity to conduct an in-depth analysis of his web presence and gain a comprehensive understanding of his business. Notably, I discovered that we shared numerous mutual connections in the industry, serving as a valuable icebreaker in our discussions.

On our scheduled call the following week, I presented a detailed analysis of his website, explaining reasons why potential customers might face challenges in locating his business online. Additionally, I shed light on their limited social media presence, emphasizing the myriad benefits of cultivating a robust online footprint.

Navigating through the sales process, addressing inquiries, and fostering a deeper understanding of their operations, we agreed to a third follow-up meeting. This session aimed to involve other key members of his team, allowing me to grasp their operational nuances and tailor a successful marketing approach through my agency's services.

Concluding the final meeting, unanimous agreement on our pricing and a commitment to move forward with the deal were reached. The result? Another client added to the roster, contributing an annual revenue of $25,000 to my business. This symbiotic relationship aimed to bolster their marketing endeavors and attract more clients.

This success story highlights the importance of remaining abreast of industry news, utilizing platforms such as LinkedIn to identify new prospective clients, and approaching them with sincere congratulations for their achievements. In this instance, a strategic approach to staying informed facilitated a beneficial collaboration, demonstrating the transformative impact of industry awareness on business development.

#11: Riches are in the Niches

In the world of agencies, a common saying is that "riches are in the niches." While it's possible to run a successful marketing agency with a broad focus, agencies that have truly thrived achieved remarkable growth by specializing in a particular industry. Think of it this way: you wouldn't hire a general practitioner for open-heart surgery, right? You'd seek out a cardiac specialist. The same principle applies when clients are searching for a marketing agency. Each company wants to partner with an agency that understands their customers and has experience in their specific industry, whether it's law, medicine, or any other field.

Reflecting on my early days in business, I tried to be everything to everyone. In the beginning, you take on any client willing to pay for your services, providing a satisfactory result. I had clients in law, medicine, real estate, and even small online stores. While it brought in money initially, after the first year and some research into what other agencies were doing, I realized the importance of finding a niche.

I recognized that the legal and medical fields were saturated with specialty agencies, making it challenging to compete. Coincidentally, two friends were starting a title insurance business around the same time. One was an experienced real estate attorney, and the other was a perpetual entrepreneur. They needed assistance with their website, social media, and online marketing, creating a natural fit for my skills.

At the time, I had bought and sold two homes, so I had a basic understanding of title insurance but wasn't an expert in the industry or its marketing needs. After conversations with my friends, the new business owners, I learned more about how title insurance companies operate. Depending on the state, title insurance is required by the buyer, and there are different policies with varying costs based on the home's purchase price. Interestingly, the homebuyer usually pays for the policy, but the real estate agent recommends the title insurance company, highlighting the importance of relationships in this industry.

Further research revealed that most title insurance companies lagged in terms of marketing, with outdated websites and minimal social media presence. Recognizing a significant opportunity for modernization and embracing digital marketing, I decided to focus on this niche.

The title insurance industry had seen little innovation, presenting a stable yet untapped market. Unlike the thousands of marketing agencies catering to the legal and medical fields, there were only a few supporting title companies. This insight led me to rebrand and position myself as a go-to agency in the title industry.

Over the next few months, I immersed myself in learning about the title industry and transformed my brand and messaging to cater specifically to this niche. I joined national and state-specific land title associations, offering webinars and sponsoring conferences. The result? The business soared over the next several years. Title companies appreciated having a specialty agency that understood their business, offering a full digital marketing team for a fraction of the cost of a full-time employee.

As I attended conferences, made connections, provided value, and delivered results, my brand and reputation in the title insurance industry grew. The key takeaway from my journey is that, in my case, the saying held true: riches are indeed in the niches. Once I positioned myself within a specific industry, the business took off, and I never looked back.

#12 Turning Passion into Profit: My Journey with Pro Shop Commerce

After experiencing 5 1/2 years of consistent growth with my agency, I found myself presented with an opportunity for an exit. In August of 2023, a national software company acquired my agency. While I assisted in the transition for the next three months, I ultimately chose not to stay on board. Instead, I wanted to continue my entrepreneurial journey and start something new.

Over the past decade, I developed a passion for golf. Despite being an athlete throughout my youth, I only delved into golf in my 30s. It proved to be a challenging sport, unlike any other I had tried before. Despite playing a few times a month, I didn't improving much until I took lessons a few years ago. Those lessons not only enhanced my game but also made golf more enjoyable. After the sale of my agency, I sought ways to combine my passion for golf with entrepreneurship.

The idea I settled on was to start a small business supporting golf courses by transforming their physical pro shops into online ecommerce stores. This concept resonated with me and a few friends I shared it with. In the US alone, there are over 10,000 golf courses, most of which have physical pro shops. However, my research revealed that very few had an attached e-commerce store. This meant that golfers visiting the pro shop often had no way to purchase course-branded merchandise unless they were on site. Recognizing this untapped potential, I envisioned helping local courses generate additional revenue and promote their brands by allowing golfers to buy merchandise anytime, anywhere, even from the comfort of their homes.

To validate my concept, I cold-called several dozen golf courses, seeking their feedback on the idea and gauging their willingness to pay for such a service. Additionally, whenever I was at a golf course over the next few months, I subtly pitched the idea to course managers, receiving positive feedback and agreement on the proof of concept. The only remaining step was to build my website and start promoting it.

In early 2024, I founded Pro Shop Commerce. As of now, I have a few clients on board, for whom we have built fully functioning ecommerce websites to sell their merchandise online. We charge a nominal fee to maintain the platform, and the results and feedback from clients have been positive. Moving forward, I plan to continue marketing and selling this service in the coming years, alongside other ventures.

The takeaway from my experience is that you can pursue your passions and find a way to turn them into a profitable venture.

Five Sales Tips to Help Grow Your Business

I want to leave you with 5 sales and business development tips that I hope will help you grow your business.

1. Know your customer – Understanding your customer is paramount in sales as it forms the foundation for building meaningful relationships and tailoring your approach to meet their specific needs. Knowledge of their preferences, challenges, and objectives allows you to position your product or service as a solution that aligns seamlessly with their goals.

This customer-centric approach not only enhances trust and credibility but also enables you to provide a personalized experience, increasing the likelihood of successful transactions and fostering long-term loyalty.

In essence, knowing your customer empowers you to articulate the value proposition effectively and create a more resonant connection that goes beyond a one-time sale.

2. Ask thought-provoking questions – Asking thought-provoking questions in sales is crucial because it encourages meaningful dialogue and helps uncover the specific needs and pain points of the customer.

These questions go beyond surface-level inquiries, prompting customers to reflect on their challenges and goals, providing valuable insights for tailoring your sales pitch. Thought-provoking questions also demonstrate your genuine interest in understanding the customer's unique situation, fostering a deeper connection and building trust.

Moreover, they allow you to position your product or service as a tailored solution, showcasing its relevance and value in addressing the customer's individual requirements. Overall, asking thought-provoking questions is a strategic approach to enhance engagement, uncover opportunities, and drive successful sales outcomes.

3. Think unconventionally – Thinking unconventionally in sales is essential because it allows you to stand out in a crowded market and approach challenges with creativity. Conventional methods may not always capture the attention of modern, diverse audiences.

Unconventional thinking enables you to identify unique solutions to problems, making your approach memorable and sparking interest. It opens doors to innovative strategies, helping you navigate changing landscapes and discover untapped opportunities.

By breaking away from traditional norms, like in the stories above, you can differentiate yourself, connect with clients on a deeper level, and find novel approaches that set you apart in the competitive world of sales.

4. Follow-up and follow-through – Fortunes are in the follow-up. Consistent follow-up is crucial in sales. After initial interactions, maintain regular communication to provide updates, answer questions, and demonstrate ongoing support. Additionally, ensure you follow through on promises made during the sales process. This reliability enhances your reputation and fosters long-term relationships with customers, potentially leading to referrals and repeat business.

5. Don't be afraid to ask for the sale – Asking for the sale is a crucial step in the sales process because it clarifies the prospect's intent and provides an opportunity to close the deal. It allows you to gauge the prospect's level of interest and address any remaining concerns or objections. Without explicitly asking for the sale, there's a risk of ambiguity, and potential clients might hesitate or delay a decision. Clear and direct communication about closing the deal demonstrates confidence and assertiveness, guiding the prospect towards a definitive decision and fostering a more efficient and successful sales process.

Conclusion:

In the dynamic scope of sales and business development, the landscape is constantly evolving. While relying on traditional norms and strategies remains crucial for success, embracing unconventional approaches can prove equally rewarding. Beyond the well-trodden paths lies an area where creativity, proactivity, and a willingness to explore the uncharted territories can yield remarkable results for your business.

Diversifying growth strategies is essential for businesses looking to thrive. This extends beyond the conventional sales and marketing playbook, opening doors to innovative approaches that resonate with a rapidly changing market. By acknowledging the need for adaptability and embracing a blend of traditional and unconventional strategies, businesses can position themselves not only to weather industry shifts but also to capitalize on emerging opportunities.

Whether it's leveraging the power of social media, exploring niche markets, or incorporating out-of-the-box marketing campaigns, the key lies in a strategic blend of proven methods and innovative thinking. Successful businesses recognize that adapting to change, staying ahead of trends, and venturing into uncharted territories can be the catalysts for sustained growth.

In essence, the path to business success is multifaceted, encompassing a spectrum of sales and marketing strategies. Embrace the evolving landscape, experiment with unconventional approaches, and let the synergy of traditional and innovative methods propel your business towards new heights.

What will the future bring for you and your business?

* 9 7 9 8 8 7 9 3 9 6 6 4 5 *